MC199BB

Published by:
PAZ Publications
P.O. Box 24100
Houston, Texas 77229-4100

Copyright © 1991 by PAZ Publications

Library of Congress Catalog Card Number
91-91287

ISBN 0-9631141-3-1

All rights reserved. No part of this publication may be reproduced or used in any form or by any means – graphic, electronic, or mechanical, including photocopying, recording, taping, or information storage and retrieval systems – without written permission of the publishers.

Manufactured in U.S.A.

First Printing, 1991.

Acknowledgments

The author wishes to thank those who assisted in the publication of this book:

J.K. Barefield, Ray Elliot, Ray Mullens & Chuck Deeter.

those who helped him believe in himself as a poet:

Christopher Carson, Audra White, Sandie Gibson,
James E. Woods, III.

those who were mentors:

Robert LeMaster, Stanley Miller, Cynthia MacDonald,
Manuel Jimenez, Bob Clark & The Firehouse Group.

those who gave great encouragement:

Madra Boyd, Ernestine Holmes, & Kirsten Newman.

Dedication

This book is dedicated to the memory of:

Mike Miesch
Doug Turner
John Bynum
Jeff Greatwood,
Jim Raub and
Manuel Jimenez . . .

. . . who believed that love could save the world . . .

Foreword

From life comes art, to celebrate itself with a manifold experience. In this understanding of what I have done, there were no options regarding the contents or style of this book; it has made itself from the material available to it, and I can make no sincere apology for the unconventionality of that stuff.

Next Erase is written in a style which seeks to minimize the use of decorative embellishments and empirical descriptions, relying instead for its art on the substantive experience of the story told. In this respect, the work of art which I present here is the book as a whole, as opposed to a collection of individual, unrelated works of art which have been combined merely for the purpose of marketing convenience. Beyond this emphasis on synergy, other innovations I have tried to utilize and/or adopt are intended to explore new possibilities for poetry as a form of art which can be more widely enjoyed by real people. First and foremost, I have attempted a book that would be entertaining.

The Author

Table of Contents:

In the Mirrors of Death

Sunday I was transplanting
spinach seedlings in the garden
chuckling to myself how
Mother would chuckle to see me now
when a shadow crossed the sun and
looking up I saw Death had come to spy on me
here in the magic garden that creates life
green things lusting for the sun and rain
thrusting in two directions to anchor earth to sky
while working here in the garden
Death has come to stand in the shadows of the sugar cane
his black shroud palpitating in the breeze
and the whole world is silent
even the wind makes no noise as
Death spies on me working in the garden –
if I should glance into his eyes...

Horizontal Fall

Always working up to that point
where nothing will stop you then
always coming near that great
jumping-off place in your mind
always thinking about
all the fine things that will be done that day
see yourself beaming after
having imagined completing every triumph
always thinking about grand designs
always waiting for that big score
take you over the top
one of these shuffles through the Big Deck
one of these rolls of the dice
always expecting the most out of every day
someday, somewhere, it may no longer elude you
always reaching for a great emptiness
arms in slow motion flail the air
body falling
horizontal.

Situation #4

They lived on one of those streets
that is 1½ lanes wide with cars parked on both sides.
When I got there I saw their neighbors
just in time –
They rolled out from behind an old buick,
she was pounding the top of his bald red head
with a piece of 2 x 4 –
I honked the horn and they got up,
walked back to the center of their front yard
where he decked her with a hard right,
she kicked him twice in the crotch, screaming.
Erma was just standing there under her mimosa tree,
fat butt just hanging out the legs of her shorts,
lawn mower just idling off to the side,
just sipping on a jumbo tumbler of ice tea.
"What's happening", I said going inside –
"Can't you tell ?", she replied.

Opening Night at the Bel Air

At the new Bel Air the restaurant is still theoretical
the physical outline of maroon and black tile
stares at you like a construction pit because
it is.
In 1974 when this was a sleaze theatre
we weren't afraid to be intimate with strangers then
now we don't really know anyone anymore
least of all ourselves –
Like two drunks trying to pass a cigarette
we reach out and waver about in the vicinity for a moment
before the thing falls, undeflected, to the ground in a perfect drop;
some strange form of awkward ballet.
In the audience tonight there are three silly girls
who laugh insanely at any mention of anal sex
but everybody knew that they really wanted it.
The two people who sit behind me
discuss a trip to Acapulco where
they plan to stay in a hotel that is classy but
not on the beach.
Like me they are disappointed the restaurant is not finished –
denied the opportunity to ostentatiously flaunt
their fake pearls and diamonds they are reduced
to discussing imaginary trips to Acapulco in
some kind of graceless last ditch effort to mean a damn
while I furtively make notes of their conversation in the dark.
Outside in the luminescence of this
suburban civilization's decay
everyone is still visibly shaken by the
slipping of the democratic mask from the face of the junta and
someone asks in a hushed tone if they'd like to
drive around and look at the christmas lights awhile.

Colony Arts Festival, Fall 1985

It rained on Saturday
but on Sunday the sun came out,
a band on bongos set the beat,
people in the crowd came out to dance,
the rest stand behind, observers of life,
from time to time one among them
sails a crumpled piece of paper money
through the air at the tip tray.
I keep just beating a group of three women
every time I go to the portacan –
I realize the third time
two of us are drinking beers at the same rate.
Down the street in front of the Liberty,
the Urban Animals on skates joust for the crowd –
The matchless knights mull about
nearby at the booths with wives, children,
helmet covered with the bones of a dog and feathers
rest in the cradle of his arm–
I approve the workmanship with a glance and a nod while passing.
No challengers will step forward from these torrents
of people floating up and down the street,
as the car of asiatic christians slowly weaves

in between the two currents, covered with slogans,
Mr. Mike prophet reaching out to the masses from behind the wheel,
cat-calls espoused from the passenger window of the shit-colored toyota.
I anoint their vehicle with beer as they cruise past
clutching their bibles like talismans,
continuing their search for lost souls on lower Westheimer.
They should know from their own experience
nobody comes here by mistake–
Not junkies for raygun nor the bus stop cassanovas,
the homicidal homophobes or the boy from Champaign,
the straights who would like to be cool for a day
but get confused and wind up threatening mayhem with an umbrella,
arguing with a gay vendor over the price of beer,
the policeman interceding at the climatic pause
that precedes the brain cycle when the animal instincts takeover,
giving them an acceptable representative of the gods to
bow to before being sent down the street,
faces still intact within the mason jars hanging around their necks.
Boys on skates, too young for battle, twist and
glide around them in parabolas;
children of turbulence, they hug the cement waves like magnets,
shooting the curve like arrows where their elders,
having failed to walk on water, now sink in concrete.

The Ritual

A time-traveler in alien dimensions
of the fields of crosses burning
white under the climbing sun
where monuments to human stupidity
crowd together as if we might run out of room for them
they speak no glories of dead heroes
but a tale those tongues could not tell
black and withered behind the stitched lips
                                        that never dissented

when told to recite their allegiance
unaware of what it would require
those of us who assumed there was nothing
                                        although too young to be heard
speaking
remembered you had liked flowers
brought them to the hole where they hid you
in the fields of crosses burning
I hear their voice also now
among the roaring flames that whisper your name
they have you back, young caesar,
who, holding life in a cup, sipped,
and must now lick flames from behind stitched lips.
You should've kept them open, brother,
you should've told them it didn't matter.

Ode to the Children of Existentialism

Why don't we ever talk about what it means ?
Why are people afraid they will stumble over the truth
and fail to understand it ?
Truth is the only thing that can be understood –
fantasy is confusion clearly we delineate
these paths like a man seeing double
every time we attempt to walk through the garden,
our ultimate horror
the fixing of a confident attitude looking forward
followed by a step off the edge of the world,
shock and surprise still gracing our faces
even after having relanded with cat-like skills,
more cautious now than even before –
How long will this walk take,
are we there yet ?

Allegretto

She loved crystals and they hung by monofilaments from her ceiling
when the sun would go down a solitary ray
fought through the matted branches outside her window
falling on a sphere suspended in the center of the room
diffracting itself into a hundred beams of rainbow light
each one arching into another crystal
splintering into separate strands of colored light
falling into still other crystals
recombining into rainbows again
returning to the sphere in the center of the room.
Long after the sky was black I watched her web of stars shining
until gradually the beams faded and then left
a single ray returning to the sun through her window into the darkness.
"If I could reach you tonight,"
she had said as we held each other's eyes,
"Who knows what new constellations might be linked together,
or from what perspectives I would return to you,
time into the future."

Beserko (part one)

Scratch Time
occupation : deliver pizza
insert spare change
this calculus oppresses me
where time = money, money = future.
In the future money will buy time
and people will ride around in gold cadillacs
driving as slow as possible
waiting to die
endless lines of gold cadillacs at the red lights
braking to a stop on the freeway on-ramps
passing away in the 11000 block of the Katy
their bodies discovered outside Schulenberg on the medians
gas tanks empty, eyes still open,
roaches urinating on the dashboard.
"Hello Dispatch this is car 54,
another roller just hit the river,
send down the divers for the watches."
There was one old man
he was driving this kind of a train
and he fell over dead out the door and
his train glided down past McKeever street
and cut this car in half and this girl inside the car
lay on the street there watching clouds go by
and heard these people talking about
she was cut in half and dead now
and she just lay there in the street watching those clouds
until they had tired of waiting for her to die

and took her to the hospital finally.
She did die a long time after that,
but it started first with the rats –
they had been eating babies for years
and then, one day, looking for special treats,
when the mayor and her council had sat down to perform,
they came screeching like banshees
millions from out of nowhere and
right there on the instant eye
ate those politicians down to the pink bone.
Beserko, part one.

Pastimes

This poem is about a man they saw looking at the stars.
He was standing on a prominence for three hours one night
before anyone noticed his strange behavior.
A skinny woman who carried an awkward box
containing all of her worldly possessions
stopped to look at the sky with him for a minute,
then picked up her box and walked away.
A passing policeman paused to talk awhile,
then left shaking his head very slowly.
Soon a crowd had gathered around the hill.
They stood staring into space, some looking puzzled,
some scratching their heads in wonder.
There was much debate as to what it could all be about.
Finally, one of them approached the man with his question,
and the man looked at him and said,
"I am making up constellations."

Sleep is Kind

What happens at night
when the eyes finally close
and when you wake up in the morning remembering nothing ?
What happens when reality stops existing ?
Sleep is restful,
sleep is kind,
but what happens at night
when you put the shutters on your mind
and live with everything trapped inside
thoughts running into each other
like winos staggering home in the early morning fog
conversing with the imaginary lampposts
on the cool quiet mornings before anyone else is awake
watching as the shift workers flip on their bedside lamps
gobble their breakfast in dimly lit kitchens
go out to warm the engines in their old work cars
rolling doobies under the dome lights
wondering why you are there
or if it is possible to really understand anything
or if you could remember all of your dreams
would you be able to live with the monsters within ?

and on the eighth day god said let there be depravity

Strike Vote

Who remembers Cadet Don and Kittrick and
their animated cartoons with the lips
that squirmed like red worms under the noses –
all the sketti-lovin' kids riding the carousel
during the steel strike when I was 5 years old –
the calloused men sitting on their haunches
standing up one by one in the circle under
the sweet gum tree in our front yard to swear
this time by god they would not go down on their knees
my sister running screaming into the house the next day
tears in her eyes Daddy's killing the rabbits
NO
Daddy is a steelworker and his friends
and his family will never go hungry
like he had to
I remember
running to the meadow on a sunny Saturday
birds singing and corny butterflies with broomstick in my hand
not strong enough to break the legs of my father
floating backwards through the air and blood flowing
from my teethmarks on the bronze forearm holding
the ball-peen hammer that fell anyway
the tiny handfuls of dirt flung just high enough
to stumble the giant cursing
Run, Lizbeth, Run
Daddy's swinging the hammer again
he's really mad now and he can hardly see
and soon the meadow must be swallowed up by the starry darkness –
Run, bunnies, Run

Red Poem

roll red waters
encroaching sea of death
rise up
over these bloody streets
over the dirty window panes
over the rotting fascia and bug-eaten joists
stain the moon with your pretty color
immerse us wash us in red
let the dance begin we are the dead –
see red
be red
do red things

Dollhouse

It was kinda like living
in a dollhouse
the panoramic vista at stage right
the precipice we must not stumble over
crossing each other in the bathroom hallway
getting up on the wrong side of the bed mornings
and the hands
the hands reach in and rearrange all the furniture on a whim
the hands drove the volks through the living room wall
and said "Hey, I'm home. What's for dinner ?"
the hands appear in mystic visions at the supper table
if only we could comprehend the sign language
the mystery of the universe might get stranger
but who would be able to understand it then ?
They were kinda like people
somehow in love
sometimes he would come home
and there would be a party waiting for him to walk in the door
sometimes he would come home
and there would be a party in progress, you know,
people got tired of waiting –
sometimes he would come home
and the party would be over
and she would be there in her best red lace Frederick's of Hollywood
slouched on the love couch swigging a bottle of gin
in the semidarkness he'd walk through the front door
her eyes gleaming red in the shadows
"Hi, Honey, I'm home."
glass shatters on the wall
"Crazy Bitch!"

nearer each time her fingernails would come to his eyes until
Fist struck Face and
Fist struck face again
a small silence before the sob
It was kinda like
prove to me you love me, you know,
it was kinda like
promise me you'll love me if I don't scream.
It was kinda like cave art, yeah,
moist and vivid images stained onto the walls
the shaman wears his deer horns and testicles chanting
"how many more seasons would these buck have balled caribou ?
who will be the first to appease the spirit of the dead ?"
People stand on the outside, smoking cigarettes, chatting,
torchlights glimmering off the stony passage walls
the next tour will start in a minute
on your left you'll see the dollhouse on Main Street
note the detail in those flower boxes underneath the busted-out windows
on your right again there is the madonna with gin bottle,
still dripping,
next the boy in leather tied spread-eagle to the bed;
all pictures of people who worshipped what they ate
it was kinda like worship, you know,
from the first provocative rub of shoulders
the humid writhing of flesh under flesh
the fingernails scraping down the curvature of his back
the quiver of pulsating muscle
please let me hit you just one more time, baby,
Fu-uH-ck Youu...
it was kinda like
trying to be majestically human, or somethin', you know,
having this idea but somehow
never coming near to approaching it.

Refrain

If I could reach out and touch your face tonight
it would not startle you
and if I could not keep my lips from touching yours
it would be a gentle kiss that I would give to you
as gentle as a summer evenings breeze
as soft as autumn leaves falling to the lawn
as long as I could stand not to look into your eyes
and wonder what you see.

Leaving Home

dust and debris
in the highway gutter
Waiting for Stormclouds

the soot-covered trees
the asbestos frame houses in rows
the streetlights shining through the haze
the dead dog decomposing in the road
has been there three days
everyone who turns this corner

runs over it again

Rolling up the Windows

dusty shell backways
winding their way past trailer-homes
light green and white
with hurricane fenced yards

it's leaving me now

the crimson-streaked and magenta sunsets
the dull glow on foggy mornings
far off on the refinery horizon
silhouettes of strange pillars with no roof

it's leaving me now

somewhere in the distance a rooster crows

Rain in the City

Today I had rain for lunch
time makes us all hypocrites growing up
one at a time
the whole world's in pain
don't need anymore pain anymore
today it rained and the short security guard at the parking garage
locked the traffic barrier in the "up" position
let everyone park inside for free
little runlets and streams of water ran
in the gutters and the sidewalks of concrete paradise
something white you can reach out and touch at 200 degrees fahrenheit
just because you want to check if it's really there
it's really there
rain runnin' all over it in dark curtains of water
carbon monoxide rainbows over the freeways
black-grey sky, thunder and lightning pitchforks
distant siren wailing in the wind
the mushy sound of tires on the road
frogs singing in the ditches
smell of wet, sensuous earth
birds chirping in the drizzle after the downpour
free showers from heaven they
bite with their beaks into their lice-infested wing-pits
and the super-heated summer asphalt steams away
tasting the steam way in the back of my nose
gold sun shining after storms passed
Loving rain in the city.

The Last Crusade

Black leather and metal-studded Children of Zeus listen to the thunder,
watch the night sky in storm waiting for a split-second.
Lightning attracts the human fascination,
but it's rain that grows food –
soaking into the burnt sienna sponge under this city
where slowly but surely
the foundations of this civilization are being shifted,
although no one ever seems to notice except the dying.
We will never be able to build prisons big enough
to force the proles to be good christians.
Born backs to the wall
bayonets to the throat
the reason people are feeling paranoid is because
everyone's out to get you:
Trust me.
Class Conflict is just like the transmission on a
1977 plymouth volare' station wagon painted green –
sometimes the gears get stuck on a mechanized society
socially engineered to talk about the great society ride:
too many to turn back now we are doomed to either
prolonging our yuppiedom cardboard existence on exercise bicycles
located on the 40th floor / free to the prisoners
chanting mindless slogans at gunpoint while awaiting braindeath by TV
or some kind of proletarian confusion:

nowhere to go, man, nothin' to do
tired of playing basketball at the youthchurch parking lot
lightning flashes in the mind
what is this strange attraction
this basic belief in the validity of psychological effects
caused by the experience of these physical sensations,
this great willingness to be okay in the face of anything,
this collective imperative to have no ills ?
We feel free, man.
We are hooked, baby, really hooked –
too many to turn back now we have no choice
but this kind of civilization or another.

When we have all finished punishing each other
for all our individual failures, what next ?

Itty Bitty Ditty

I am man,
see me stand
high on two legs two eyes watchin'
saw what was comin', and ran.
I am man,
see me ride
high in the sky like a silver dragonfly
down in the sea in the green sea-weed
steamin' up the twin tracks
and skiing down the freeways,
I am man,
watch me comin',
see me go.

Puncturality

Long blue fingers open and close on air
like frog legs kicking in Dr. Scorrow's lab
they long to have and to hold in that grasp
to pull closer in as if this would
complete some action of knowing
something once taken for granted
in prior consciousness a priori
now connected to the holes in the wall
now detached and motionless, poised,
now connected to the holes in the wall
now frozen stiff, cocked like a pistol,
now connected to the holes in the wall
now statuesque, numb with the creeping blueness,
this fist is not broken yet.

Second Feeling in the Asylum of Souls

No manifestos tonight
No sermons on grammatical etiquette or
the need for concrete imagery
I am tired of solid objects
blocking my view
attacking my face
with the obscenity of neon lights
blinking their moronic slogans
and filling space with the confusion
of their mutual proximity and juxtaposition.
Yesterday I was walking down I-10 East
when looking up I suddenly noticed
all the cars were traveling in reverse
all of the people smiling and waving good-bye to me
but I didn't stop walking
and I didn't run after them
I didn't even blink my eyes
it was, in fact, only several days later
that it occurred to me someone might find this strange and novel
and I only mention it now to demonstrate
that I'm sick of the confusion
disgusted with the stupidity
Your pain makes me puke
because you are obsessed with it's experience
and because it is the only thing you choose to share
but most of all because I am too weary to feel for you anymore
or even care about my own hypocrisy and guilt.
Looking back I understand now that giving you compassion
was like trying to irrigate the desert with a single pail of water.

Time and time again I have watched you from eye-level
in with the crowds of people rushing to beat the crowds of people
stuck in the traffic, trapped in the interstices
between workaday and home in the village
lunging forward inches at a time like columns of deranged turtles
like lemmings driving to the sea
like ants carrying leaf-chips to and fro
yet we comprehend our lives are dominated by Death;
we slow down to gaze impassively at the carnage
now even the geysers of blood and bits of gut
that explode out of a stomach spinning like pinwheels
are not interesting to us anymore.
Exactly what's at stake in this effort we make
to control time in the animal city ?

We are all mad.

We go through the motions and play the charade
we say the lack of meaning doesn't bother us anymore
we pretend to be living but inside we are dead

and you know it.

Like the winos on Market Street
we swagger around with our empty bottles in brown paper bags
telling everyone we have a little piece of God in there,

just in case.

This is sufficient to enslave humanity:
give them social positions, niches to habitate within

the System.

The occupation is trying to make it to next payday
and if the circumstances make you feel insecure
someone can sell you insurance.

Friday Night

So there you are with your empty tin cans
all opened with the label right-side-up
no cans opened from the bottom around here
sure there's no difference but
why would anyone deliberately she is thinking unless
one mindlessly stacks cans in the pantry up-side-down
or habitually flips everything over
to find delight in the craziness of bizarre practices.
Time makes us all heroes in strange ways,
unexpectedly.
So here I am with my crazy little habits,
burning sofas, wrecking cars, never working,
you must remember it's just my manly faults
that made me so irresistible to you in the first place.
Irresistible.
What if little by little she had
lost all power to resist the temptation until
there was nobody left to refuse consent
the identity sucked out of the body like
a spider queen sucks her prey
the husk of his being
mechanically functional
the only thing that mattered now–
what's in it for you ?
Clocking the different levels on a liquor bottle becoming empty
watching melancholy late at night motionless
while the knuckles are blistered on my unconscious hand still
clenching the lit cigarette
4 AM
no fire alarms ringing.

Monsters in the Audience

The Speaker has begun with the contention
certain people are just incompetent
when it comes to social interaction.
He demonstrates the theory
placing his big toe in his mouth and falling on his butt
some of the colleagues are amused but don't really understand;
he gathers his thesis together in the embarrassed silence.
I try too but sometimes still don't get it.
Later that night at the Great Fame City Bar Debate
JJ and the Earth Woman have united
in a preference for scotch over vodka against him,
arguing the employee who is prescribed lithium
is a problem they must solve
the only way they know how.
Heroically he inquires if they would do this
to a person with one leg and they answer
you can lose a leg and still be human.
People think they are so smart,
monsters aren't stupid.
There are none of us ever completely independent
my Mom told me once over the telephone
the night after I had left her house forever
still a baby monster.
JJ will be forty-five next week but
still later that evening at Earth Woman's
she has raised her clenched fists into the air
explaining how her mother has ruined her life forever again.
I don't understand what makes you people tick
I can't comprehend the way you want to think and
all of my poetry are lies to you.

From Out of the Blue

I came from out of the blue and was
not without reflection on the void,
the abyss within –
If expression has become characterized by passage
from one frame of reference to the next,
and if the experience of emptiness cannot be completed
until the emptiness becomes fulfilled,
who will remain to contrive art-like history
when the patterns become disestablished ?

One Moment / March 6, 1988

I couldn't be sinister with a slate blue file cabinet
on sale 49.99 save $10, caddy w/casters 9.99
18" deep with key lock
in the living room it would stand
obliquely, in that area, restricting access to the
shop manuals, telephone, and sex movies,
into her 4 gorgeous stomachs go all the writing
when she is gorged, turn the key, turn the key,
bury all my twisted and deformed children in the slate blue cow
hide them, hide them, a pedestrian and his wife the accoutrement
desire to stroll this block near dusk and
cannot bear to see them wading on their stumps in the tepid ditches
feeling for crawfish, diving for frogs
and I like a Taiwanese wind chime on the porch
tinkling with the awkward emotions stirred by a misbegotten progeny –

Oh, to make a thing of beauty

Doghouse

My father has fastened upon a simple design
of classic lines his stiff and unfacile hands
are well-practiced at hewing with crude tools
of his own evolution and honor:
his honesty leaves no confusion
this thing he is thinking of making is a doghouse.

Obsession

When you look at something, do you see it ? He has obsessed me since that night; not an exceptionally handsome or well-built young man, but that smile had magic to it, those eyes had sparkled with enthusiasm. I have tried since then first to put him completely out of mind or alternately to find him again, but can do neither. Was it the years of adolescent conditioning under the heel of heterosexual domination that led me to walk away that night ? Insidious is that training of the mind to hide the truth even from itself. Stopping for a hamburger once I imagined it was his voice that took the order only to find a stranger at the pick-up window. Another time I thought I saw from the corner of my eye his face peering over the balcony across the street. Yet again last night it was his shoulders that slept under my arm until morning, when the sun rose on unfamiliar features.

The Reading Bible

I have found your reading bible
hidden under the tree in the garden
question marks in the margins
while you were out cruising Sunday Boulevard
a little sip of the convertible sweet life for you
I masticated this and the noises you had made to me
grinding the spoken words into digestible pulp
savoring every bitter flower and poison root
that has been flung before me like fodder
incredible new lies encompassing previous lies
vast subterfuges betrayed by innocence and cunning
substitution of details
omissions
I really hate it when people fail to lie cleverly
as if your deception were, after all, essentially unimportant:
There will be no bargain this time to remain silent
and be allegedly deceived.
You have to understand
Dealing with Liars is not love;
Only Love can be Honest
Only Truth can be Free
Fear is the silent lie I have believed
every time I have longed to taste your alkaline passions once again.

and there you were still
in the long cold night
after the moon had broken

Bird Underground

I like young people because they're always making
these plans for the future like someday I'm gonna be
and we just are
freefalling
nowhere to land
always coming down
long time ago I was gonna be
sometimes I still think
I can learn how to fly
soar up out of this hole
find the sun again and
leave him behind
forget I ever loved his smile
forget I ever missed his haunting eyes.

Boy at Dance

So you're telling me you can't but you know it's a lie
anyone can dance
what you're saying is you're not better at it than others
and you don't do things your not better at
which is too bad because
you have to dance alot of bad dances to get good but
this avoids the point: it's a matter of carefree physical expression.
Didn't you know I'm afraid of love also ?
Last night I saw you looking at me across the ballroom floor
beyond the glitter and lights on the other side of this small universe
Last night you saw me looking at you but
I couldn't look long
I can't look too long in eyes like yours
they draw me in
it's the same feeling I get on the 24th floor
looking over the balcony's railing it draws me
falling I lunge backwards pulse racing
grabbing for something solid
freezing in life like a momentary rabbit on the freeway
transfixed before those glaring headlights before
breaking visual contact to scramble for the bushes.
I don't know what to do about it.

Archaeopteryx

Hear me fine-grained rock that closes tightly around my hollow bones
be worn away by that patter of rain
I have heard coming nigh for many centuries
be dissolved and carried away to oceans
that await your jurassic sediments on the other side of the world
if I should see the golden sun blink again through chink or crevice
then I know I shall be free
from this choking desperation.

Boy with Wings

First there is something about the way he
remembers Descartes that makes you smile,
inversing the existential statement.
Something believably innocent about the way he
believes innocence to be almost universal,
something embracing about those eyes,
hound-puppy eyes with brows furrowed in
some calculation on how to divide 3 ice cream cones –
he is like suddenly being surprised with cookies and hot chocolate
on a nippy November Saturday in some other life.
He wants to talk about Monterrey, Woodstock, Altamont,
Watergate, Vietnam, the days they shot Martin, Bobby, John;
he remembers these things 10 years differently if at all,
it is like some kind of celestial compass
he uses to get his bearings on you.
You know 10 years from now that difference won't matter to anyone.
He says he has a poster of Jim Morrison.
You imagine it hangs on back of his bedroom door.
He wears whimsical sunglasses on colored string and polo shirt
two sizes too large hanging just to the top of his thighs.
You think he is too self-conscious, defensive, aloof
about that body for nineteen years old.
You see nakedness unseen by woman.
Under the table your foot has stroked his instep and
the eyebrows arch.

You wonder if there have been, or are, girlfriends;
a nice catholic girl who writes corny love poems and
owns a hope chest filled with quilts made by Granny.
A heavy metal tomboy who rode dirt bikes and
drank Jack Daniels out of the bottle.
A ballet dancer in the suburbs who rides her sunny bicycle
Saturday mornings past a pond filled with ducks.
Their collective puzzlement at his physical remoteness.
His own guilt for being different and adolescent and
still trying to make sense of it all . . .

Targets

I believe in letting things grow
I have no need to control the grass
all my neighbors think I am a bad person.

Just look at that yard
even the trees look wild there
the lawncut boys throw their beer cans in my ditch.

White Trash
I believe in freedom
I come home from work
there are bullet holes in the windows
strange phone calls at night
we know you are a goddam faggot
click.

I believe in faggotry
I like to watch the wild animals in the yard
bunny rabbits, squirrels, possums, woodpeckers, frogs
I keep a loaded weapon at the ready
Click
anytime you feel lucky, sister.

Coming of Age

what is this thing that is called a man ?

a man is a little boy that has grown up
learning that the world is prepared
to strip from him everything he is not willing to fight for
and a man is a boy who knows
that it is the strong who take the weak
that it does not help to cry or feel sorry
or to feel anything sometimes
you go numb

so many things are done for the first time...

Matrix One

Ain't it funny how people never die in dreams.
I mean they'll fall off the top of something
but never hit the ground. In the dream.
It's like deep inside we know we're doomed but
it's just too awful to ever really think about –
what it would feel like to die; be dead. Stink.
So we don't. We don't think about that. We know but
it's just too awful. Deep inside the human mind there is
this basic willingness to be dishonest to feel good.
People just like to feel good. Okay. Right now.
Look at little kids who tell ridiculous lies.
The spaceman from Mars broke the famous vase.
They're not smart enough to realize this lie is ridiculous,
but they are smart enough to know how to lie.
People learn to lie even before they know how to think,
people lie to avoid thinking, people think to lie.
I don't know what it means. People never die in dreams.
To thine own delusion be true.
Maybe all of this is maya maybe
any concept of self as separate from godhead,
maybe even nibbana is just another level of dishonesty.

Backlash

something happens when
you can't see their faces
the photograph resurfaces
the back of an uncleaned drawer
don't take pictures unless
you want to walk with ghosts also
don't talk about places that used to be
or events that have lost all their memories but yours
don't read newspapers they're all writing about
we the innocent nazi sluts are dying now also;
yes, it's a wild and sinister world, girl,
look out for that nuclear bomb, John.

Donuts

I wanted to tell you about
all of the things that are said
with glances of the eye
that day we were in the donut place
where I didn't want to be because you eat like a pig
but the hairy ape cycling by on the sidewalk
has your complete attention and
anger found sarcasm handy so
I'm saying instead you should wave at him
run outside and give him your number
if you think he would slow down long enough
to let a fat toad like you catch up on foot.
People sometimes are just
incompetent when it comes to social interaction,
never do or say the right things
except by accident or cosmic astrological intervention –
it is my natural condition to fail to understand,
stop dying, goddammit.

Corner

Sons of Daedalus and Archimedes built this place
with levy, pulley, fulcrum they
raised the tall houses and made the city a labyrinth
streets that bleed under mercury-vapor lights
no one else watching as the puddle enlarges
flows to the curb in a thick syrup
before the street cleaners in their scrub-brush buggies
grind down the gutter lanes polishing the edges
to a lighter tone of dingy grey spackled with
faint blotches of pink, fading memories of darkness
so black, so endless, so paralytically engulfing
I have often felt there was no way out.

Thread

sooner or later he was bound to stumble across it again
remember everything
follow it backwards everywhere it had led him
crazed now like Theseus having
beaten the Minotaur to death with his fists
follow it backwards to Ariadne,
worriedly holding one hand in the other across her breast,
waiting for her adolescent lover to return from the darkness...
There is never any returning.
Every moment, every motion in a lifetime of spinning
happens once, and forever...
What's in it for you, babe ?
You're a bit too old to pass yourself off
as some kind of nut that is just attracted
to being the last one to go down with the ship –
Am I wearing the last life jacket in the bar here
or is there something else you wanted to say before...
was it like they said, that I felt attracted to him because
the act of doing that perpetuated the notion I was trash or because
he was so much like I used to be I was really
just in love with my own youth or vicariously
doing it all over a second time to avoid growing up –
he had changed me, it was true; ran with the younger crowd now,
just like old times in some ways but
back then I was just fooling around, hanging out...

Dear John,
your mother and sister made you a very nice panel for the quilt
I went to see it in D.C. and in Houston
it was the kind of saccharine bullshit you would've hated
so I didn't think you'd mind if I left it to them
you would've died laughing at the mess I was struggling with before...

snap.

Dog Wagging in the Park

Dear John,
there is another boy now
it turns out I've known him for quite some time
but never let myself feel anything
I have not been letting myself feel anything
for a long, long time now,
and you are just dead.
I suddenly realized that the other day
I had gone down to the park we went on Sundays
and there was one of these stray dogs
such as the ones that always ran
tail wagging across the green when they saw you coming
but you weren't there the other day and
the dog came running, tail wagging, up to me.
You're just dead and
we can't talk about it anymore.

Snow for the First Time

In February 1973 it snowed
two times in one month in Houston
the second time two inches of fuzzy ice swirled
over the flat landscape in ripples
adhering to the uppermost branches of trees.
Schools were of course closed and
every kid in Houston was outside in the streets
real snowmen clutching
sugar cane fishing poles
out on the fairway
some of the moms with their
thermos full of toddies venture out around ten
to instigate snowball world war 3
when the sun had finally begun to go down
a frost-bitten sadness filled the whole world
somehow we knew even if it snowed again
which it hasn't
it would never really be the same.

Boy with Shoes

The advertising supplement that serves as this week's coaster says
save 20% on dress and casual shoes to add to
your walking wardrobe.
There are always those moments you remember,
who knows why they stick.
I recall one particular Saturday
we sat up all night watching MTV
because he thought this was romantic,
so I'm sitting there on this couch, 4:30 AM,
watching him do sit-ups;
he wanted so bad to be butch like James Dean for awhile
but then he finally got a job and
they told him he was going to sell ladies pumps.
You have to understand with an employee discount
and a few strategic clearance sales
a girl can afford alot of nice shoes;
so much for James Dean.
You have to understand I was not there in the beginning
it wasn't my fault I just felt
when he was anywhere near
and when I was far I just felt
it was partly my fault, too,
but I did not care at first
you have to understand nobody thinks about desire
some people can't feel desire anymore
and they say this is wisdom

maybe the desire for wisdom makes even old people fools
maybe mistakes are nothing to regret
maybe we're all just fools any way you cut the deck
you have to understand fascination is not love
you have to understand I know
I am not a real person in this situation
that I have no real value in
his little algebra of the universe;
save time, save money, save the whales
but never save love for the boy
who has bought his walking shoes.

Wit's End

At wit's end
we are all at the mercy of God.

Philosophical Bag-Ladies
too depraved to even realize
our precious possessions must look like
sacks of silly garbage
the ones with the heaviest bags the most insane,
yet those with less idolize these above everyone else,
who's the craziest then ?
Everybody's writhing in pain,
the whole world is twisted up into this ball and
gnawing on a rubber band...

5 o'clock

What am I doing here
Why do I make my life into freeway dogfights
stretched out hundreds of miles into
hundreds of thousands of miles and
a servant to the unreasonable demands of
my masters the sharkmen
a remora for the little shreds of skin that
float away from the red cloud of their survival
day in, day out,
it bothers me.

no more. no more. why not say it,
but what then ?
a plan that never materializes,
another Friday night with cigarettes, coffee, typewriter.
I steal their pens to jot these words,
it's a bad trade.

Creativity Becomes Infinite

Poetry is like the river
we live it in flow
always reaching for a great beyond
one day we rush into the sea
sometime in the future our
molecules evaporate into atmosphere
drift back over land and
fall softly on green petals
soak into the ground and
flow under
flow over
Creativity Becomes Infinite
stirs us with a flickering
we stretch ill-conceived pseudopods
like starving amoebas to encompass
things moved away
always flowing forward
always reaching for a great beyond...

Matrix 2B

What is it about life that makes us ignore death,
or at best answer it with a kind of gibberish,
a grand denunciation that finally falls on deaf ears ?

Does the day comprehend the night, the waking mind the dream,
or is it true the cows so loved humankind they
willingly sacrificed their lives to create hamburger meat ?

Yet does the caterpillar comprehend the butterfly, the acorn sturdiness,
or any form of being we see change understand it's future,
and having been transformed forgotten it's own past ?

Where is this wall, this boundary, this line of separation between
being and nothingness, nothingness and transformation,
can the shaman turn to raven, is the exclusive value of life in life?

What is it about life that makes us ignore death,
or at best answer it with a kind of gibberish,
a grand denunciation that finally falls on deaf ears ?

The Empty Cup

In the Garden there are many paths
and even knowledge is but another form or level of desire;
desire that bonds us together into society,
desire that we feel most acutely when alone.
We have become human to walk the paths of desire,
to learn disappointment from experience;
we walk these paths to reach the river,
there are no short-cuts or free rides.
It is not wrong to pursue desires,
nor could any transformation occur in one who
has not drained the cup first.

One day, while standing in the back yard,
the notion occurred to me that in all the cosmos
there could only be one soul.